LIFE'S LIL JOURNEYS

Lil tips for my

Lil Brothers

LIFE'S LIL JOURNEYS

Lil tips for my

Lil Brothers

Melvin J. Stevenson

MJ'S Personal Motivator Books
Phoenix, Arizona

LIFE'S LIL JOURNEYS
Published by:
MJ'S Personal Motivator Books
P.O. Box 60521
Phoenix, Arizona 85082
Phone: 602-793-5776
Melsmotivation@aol.com

Melvin J. Stevenson, Publisher/Editorial Director
Yvonne Rose/QualityPress.info, Book Packager

All Rights Reserved.

No part of this book may be used, reproduced or transmitted in any form or by any means —electronic or mechanical, including photocopying, recording or by any information storage and retrieved system without written permission from the publisher, except for the inclusion of brief quotations in a review or critical article.

MJ'S Personal Motivator Books are available at special discounts for bulk purchases, sales promotions, fund raising or educational purposes.

Copyright © 2017 by Melvin J. Stevenson
ISBN #: 978-1-937269-67-8

Dedication

To the single mothers raising their boys to men I dedicate this to you and hope that some of my life's experiences may guide and help your sons.

Contents

Dedicated i

Preface v

PART ONE

9-12 YEARS OF AGE —————————————— 1

1 : Household Responsibilities ------------------ 3

2 : Respect Yourself ------------------------------ 6

3 : Grooming Yourself --------------------------- 8

PART TWO

13-16 YEARS OF AGE ————————————— 15

4 : Being a Gentleman --------------------------- 17

5 : Showing Respect ----------------------------- 19

6 : Education --------------------------------------- 21

7 : Saying No To Drugs and Alcohol ---------- 25

8 : Puberty --- 28

PART THREE
17-21 YEARS OF AGE —————————— 31

9 : Dealing with Others —————————— 33

10 : Your 1st Job —————————————— 35

11 : Financial Management ——————— 37

12 : Continuing Your Education ————— 40

Conclusion ———————————————— 42

About the Author ———————————— 43

Preface

To my young brothers of the world. I write these pages with hopes and wishes. Read it with an open mind and a willingness to understand.

PART ONE

9-12 years of age

Notes

1
Household Responsibilities

Hello fellas. At this point, you are probably wondering why someone would address me with ideas of how to take care of my household responsibilities. The reason being is that you know in your heart that your mom has left or given you a list of things to do. What I would like to share with you is the possibility of doing those things without being told to do so, i.e.: making your bed, keeping your room clean, taking out the garbage (throughout the house) doing your homework, and least- liked washing

Life's Lil Journeys

the dishes after dinner, walking the dog, or just picking up after yourself in general. As you can see the list can go on and on. That's why I want to share my life experiences with you, so that you can have some skills to work these things to your advantage, as well as helping your mother take on her daily chores. Remember, you are family and a family that does things together supports one another to stay together.

Remember the word 'attitude'. If you were to put the numbers of the coordination letter to numbers of the alphabet and add them up you would come up with 100, that's right, attitude =100%. If your attitude is right, that 100% of effort you put towards doing what you know you ought to do, believe me brother, you mom's attitude towards you will change greatly, and to your benefit. Some things I listed in the previous paragraph. I am going to touch on them shortly. First things first.

Responsibilities towards yourself, towards your family; and if you have no siblings, then we direct it back to your mother, which makes up your immediate family.

As a Young man, your mother is trying to teach you, at a young age; so that when you do get to

Household Responsibilities

the place in life when you have to think for yourself, you will know right from wrong. In the word responsible I like to use a word link that's spelled out: Response-Able. You are able to respond to your responsibilities, according to the know-how of what you have learned. You see, life is a continual learning cycle; once you stop learning, you stop growing and in order to grow, you must obtain knowledge and wisdom. Something that will be discussed in other life's little journeys. So there you have it, plain, simple and in black and white. Remember, we all have choices and the choice we make we are held responsible for.

2
Respect Yourself

Sounds like that song, sung by the family, The Staple Singers. It has a special ring to it. Sounds like though it's saying, *if you respect yourself, others will too*. When you carry yourself with pride and dignity, not cockiness, or acting like you're Mr. Tuff guy. Simply walking with your shoulders upright and your head held with confidence. When you speak, you expect to be heard or listened to. I can assure you the same thing goes on in your mother's head when she speaks to you. "Does this boy even hear me?"

Household Responsibilities

"Son, are you listening to what I'm telling you?"
Listen to me when I'm talking to you."

I'm sure we've heard it a thousand times; when in actuality, you ignored her, not meaning any harm or disrespect. You just simply didn't listen to what she was saying; yet when you speak, you expect people or your mother to listen, right? There you have it, don't play like you didn't hear her, the most respectful thing you as a Young man can do is one of the two things. Reply to her in a respectful manner and tone of voice or get up and go see what she wants. You never know, she may have a surprise or gift for you. Because you were so thoughtful and took out the trash, made up your bed and washed the dishes and doing your homework without her having to tell you so. Remember, in order to get it, you have to be willing to give it.

3
Grooming Yourself

As a young man from the ages of 9-12 years, you should have the basic concept of keeping yourself clean.

The word groom means:

1st Make neat, attractive or acceptable

2nd Clean and care for

3rd One who cleans and brushes

Grooming Yourself

This means several things I am going to try and make this as simple as possible, because it is. I mean to keep yourself clean and groomed is very simple, yet a lot of young men have the tendencies (to act in a particular way) to forget about the simple things. Remember this and you will have and keep in control of your personal hygiene (groom). We will break the body down into three areas, paying particular attention to those areas broken down.

Plain and simple, the head: Hair, depending on your hair style and your ethnic group (relates to race or people with common customs), you should wash your hair daily. Those of you that are Afro-American should be aware of your daily activities. If you are involved in physical activities that cause you to perspire and sweat, you should at least be rinsing your hair in the shower. Be careful as to not wash your hair daily because it will eventually dry your hair out. Afro-Americans tend to have oily skin and use hair grease. Therefore, by rinsing and not shampooing daily, the ingredients from the shampoo will not remove all the oil substance from your hair causing it to become dry and brittle. According to your style of hair, your hair grease should be able to be washed out and rinsed thoroughly.

- **G**-Stands for **Good Washing**-showering daily a minimum of once daily and twice if necessary.

- **R**-Stands for **Refreshing**-smell and clean fresh scents.

- **O**-**Odor** - no body odor - if you can smell yourself, it's likely that others can too.

- **O**-**Outstanding** habits cause good general cleanliness

- **M**-**Manage** - do what's necessary and appropriate to keep yourself clean and presentable. Mouth-teeth another important area - remember to rinse your mouth with an antiseptic mouth wash for at least 30 seconds, then brush for a minimum of 1 to 2 minutes, also when brushing, don't forget to brush your tongue. This helps eliminates bad breath. Also, flossing after eating and before bedtime, and rinsing your mouth again before bed helps eliminate odors that can

Grooming Yourself

come from bacteria being left overnight. Remember, if you can taste or smell a foul odor from yourself, its highly possible that someone else can too. What's the first thing you usually notice when you meet a person? Their smile.

The body, also known as the torso or trunk, arms, underarms, chest, stomach and hands. What we are describing is the actual body.

- **B**-bathe daily - at least once a day and before going to bed. When washing your body try to use shower gels. They prevent drying out the skin and help in keeping the shower from having soap scum stains.

- **O**-Odor - keep your body odor-free yet use colognes sparingly. You don't want to overdo it. However, you do want your body to be welcoming.

- **D**-Deodorant - as you grow and develop, your body will change. Start using deodorant and pay attention, as to whether they work or not. If you start perspiring, that is if sweat starts rolling down from your underarms, it's more than likely a sign saying *try another brand*.

- **Y-**your body - nobody knows you like you do. Listen to and take care of yourself. As you grow, your body will take on changes. So, watch those changes and adjust to them accordingly.

Another area to remember is taking care of your hands and nails. (Manicure) the easiest way to do this is, after taking a shower or while in the bathtub. File your nails, clip them if necessary to a neat trim appearance.

Also, lotioning your body keeps your skin from getting dry. The best time to apply hand and body lotion is after drying off, but not to a complete dry. Leave your body damp a little and also when drying your body pat your skin dry. The moistness of your body will absorb the lotion easier and keep your skin refreshed and smooth.

Legs and feet: When getting out of the shower and or bathtub, pat dry your skin, apply lotion to your legs and feet. Applying lotion to your feet

Grooming Yourself

is a good thing; it keeps them soft and moist. Remember to apply lotion to the heels of your feet and also to the toes, again. Keep your toenails trimmed and or filed. Do not be afraid to walk around barefoot sometimes, or wear socks after lotioning your feet, this will keep them moist. Remember, it's your body and no one likes stinky feet. So, take care of them now and you'll avoid getting or catching athlete's feet. (Fungus of the feet, dry and cracking). Changing your socks daily and after playing keeps them aired out.

There you have it, a short journey of taking care of yourself and some responsibilities. If you have questions, don't be afraid to ask your mother. She probably will be glad you did because she didn't know how to approach you about certain things or issues. When you openly communicate, you make it easier for others, including your mother, to communicate with you. Until next time, do what's right.

PART TWO

13-16 years of age

Notes

4
Being a Gentleman

Have you ever heard the saying, *"You're a gentlemen and scholar?"* If you have, I can imagine how that made you feel. Actually, it was a compliment not to be taken lightly.

When someone notices your well-mannered behavior, it makes you feel proud of yourself. Well in this topic we are going to talk about being a gentleman. **Webster** has it as *"A man of good family or manners."* When someone pays

Being a Gentleman

you a compliment like that, they are telling you that you are acting and being well mannered; it is another way of saying you are being respectful, polite and courteous.

This is where I would like to share my thoughts and points of view towards the opposite sex. That's right, girls or ladies. Gentlemen, when dealing with the opposite sex, at your age, you should be acting or conducting yourself as if that young lady were your sister or close relative. Therefore, no hitting and pushing, or shoving, as well as calling her out of her name. There is simply no place acceptable for it in a gentleman's character. When playing around or joking, you should always be conscious of what you are about to say or how you are going to say it. I cannot express this enough. There is simply no reason for acting or being disrespectful. The key being, treat that lady or girl as you want the next gentlemen to treat your sister or mother.

5
Showing Respect

That goes toward your elders (*Adults*) - your parents, and anyone older than you. Be it that man down the street, your teacher and or a friend of the family. It should be yes sir, no sir, yes ma'am, no ma'am, thank you, no thank you, and you're welcome. The main thing here is that you be consistent (*steady and regular*).;

Life's Lil Journeys

Another point to add, when answering the phone is to be courteous and polite. Always answer with a smile in your voice. People can literally hear it. When answering, be patient and listen, get the correct name and telephone number. Ask if you may take a message or ask who is calling. Respect is one of the character traits that will take you far in life's journeys.

- **R**-stands for remember to do unto others as you would have them do unto you.
- **E**-stands for Everybody plays a part.
- **S**-stands for Showing it to receive it.
- **P**-stands for Politeness and Purposeful.
- **E**-stands for Everyone's personality is different.
- **C**-stands for Control your emotions.
- **T**- stands for Totally giving and receiving respect.

There you have it again, respect overall. Give it and you will receive it. Something that will follow you in life.

6
Education

I know we've all heard it before. Get an education and you can go places and do things. Well my brother, I have to agree with your mother on this one. The one thing that has power is education. No one can ever take that away from you. Once you have learned something of value, you can use it to your advantage. Take a look at today's society, computers, technology, math, reading, science and natural raw talents. All of them go together to make up who and what you will be about. Take a moment to look at your life on *what you are learning… and are you learning with an open mind?* Your mind is like a sponge. Right now, eager and quick to grasp the basic concepts of everything. Pay attention when you're in school because later on in life it's going to pay off. Learn all that you can. It's amazing how you can become an overall brilliant young man. I am talking about the basic fundamentals of going through life: Math, Spelling, Science, Reading and Writing. You will amaze yourself, if you give yourself 15-minutes a day reading some type of educational, or inspiring material. You would eventually become well-read.

Know how to multiply, subtract, do fractions and percentages, in your head with ease and you will see how easy other situations come to you naturally. As you start learning basic concepts of education and how it can benefit you, try to start focusing on your natural God-given talents. *Put the two together and man, watch out.* When you start doing things that you have a knack for and

Education

the education is there to support you, ***Brother the sky is the limit***. So, in so many words, what I am trying to convey to you is, use your educations along with your God-given talents and watch how you eventually find what you love to do. That will land you possibly into your career decision. Please, from one brother to another, don't ever lose sight of this!

- **E**-Evaluate what it is you want to become in life.
- **D**- Do what is necessary to learn.
- **U**-Uniqueness - there is something special in you.
- **C**-Career is whatever you want it to be.
- **A**-All things are possible.
- **T**-Time you can squander or use it wisely
- **I**-Individual go within to find the magic you seek.
- **O**-Options or choice - you have to decide which one.
- **N**-Never give up - just when you think it's over something comes through.

Learn as much as you can while you can. Educate yourself and know thyself. By knowing who you are and what you want out of life, you will lead a purposeful life...not playing second fiddle to someone else's tune.

7

Saying No To Drugs and Alcohol

Brother, one of your biggest and most difficult tasks will be that of being able to say no, that is, to drugs, alcohol and or cigarettes. Some of your friends will offer it to you or even try to get you to sample it, so you can be part of the crew or click. What we call this is *peer pressure*. You know it's not right, so don't do it. Especially if you're out with some people you've just met, "run into" "been introduced to" you can save yourself and you mom a lot of grief, worry, heartache and misery. Not only will you save yourself from troubles, however; when doing drugs or drinking at such a young age, your brain has not fully developed. Therefore, you are selling yourself short of the opportunity to learn and be creative. Remember, when your mind is clear, you think clearer. Doing or trying drugs is simply no good.

I suggest asking your mother if you're curious, or better yet, don't do it. We as adults know what you're up to. Don't try to be sneaky about it. Just ask. Remember, open communication can avoid a lot of trouble later on. Besides that, it's against the law for you, as a minor, to purchase and or have someone purchase it for you. I truly believe that if you ask questions to the right adult, figure they will help you find answers to your questions. The bottom line is simply - do drugs, do time. Say no to drugs and yes to life.

- **D-Dopey**
- **L-Love**
- **R-Rude**
- **I-Inspiring**
- **U-Ugly**
- **F-Full of potential**
- **G-Gross (vulgar)**
- **E-Excitement**
- **S-Stupid**

Live your life with a clear mind and a clear conscience. Have you or do you know someone who is always looking over their shoulder? Jumping or being startled when someone walks from behind? This is not the kind of lifestyle you or anybody should be living. Enjoy your life to the fullest and let your mind and brain flourish to its full potential.

8
Puberty

Oh yeah, we have to talk about this. The subject that is so lovely and beautiful that some people are afraid to discuss it. As a young man, your body is beginning to change, which it probably has already. As a mentor and friend. I am going to explain this with an open mind.

If you are being sexually active, you should know the proper use of contraceptives (condoms) and birth control. The most respectful thing you

Puberty

could and should be doing is abstinence. That's right! Hold on to your virginity until you have grown comfortable with who you are and who you would like to share that experience with. Do not carelessly give yourself away, cherish that special moment and place and time. It will be worth the wait. Having your first sexual experience could be something to cherish or regret. Get to know who you are, and more importantly, know your potential partner even more. By doing so, not only do you put off the possibility of regretting a major turnaround in life with the chance of an unwanted pregnancy, the possibility of a sexually-transmitted disease (STD), and or receiving or contracting herpes or the AIDS virus. As you can see, the chances are greatly increased by the risks you take. Almost like playing Russian roulette, not worth the chance. Okay enough of the scary stuff, because let's face it, it's scary. Puberty is growing to know you.

- **P**-patience - good things come to those who wait.
- **U**-Understanding who you are and what you are about.
- **B**-Becoming your own young man.
- **E**-Everyone you know has the capability of influencing and or encouraging your decision- making; so make your own choices.
- **R**-When you have matured, the time will be right listen to your inner-thoughts; they will guide you.
- **T**-Time - the most precious thing we have, use it wisely.
- **Y**-Youth, remember and cherish your childhood; you can never get it back. Enjoy it while you're young. Try not to grow up too fast.

There it is, real simple. Life is a challenge. A challenge that can be enjoyed by relishing the decisions you make. Remember that saying your mom had said before*," you make your own bed; you'll have to lay in it."* Meaning living with the choice you make, good or bad.

PART THREE

17-21 years of age

Notes

9
Dealing with Others

Alright, here we go. Let's keep it simple. Let's start with some sayings that we've probably heard of before, i.e.: "Do unto others as you would have them do unto you!" I remember as a youth, my dad changed it up on me and said, "Do for others as you will have them do for you."

Dealing with Others

A little different approach, however very effective. "You get what you give out most of the time." It's as if you do before asking someone to do for you. Then, that way it's easier for people to want to help or do something in return for your act of kindness or generosity.

As you get older in life, your way of appreciating things and your lifestyle will begin to change and, hopefully, for the better. When dealing with others, how about always remembering or acting with kindness and love. I like the old saying," Be loving and kind to each and one another." Recall the Beatles song "All we need is love!"

When dealing or asking something of one another, "You get more with honey than you do with vinegar." Try to develop a pleasing personality, smile more often, listen when someone is talking, and let them finish their thoughts. Be genuine and true to yourself, as well as others. People make the world go round, we can all get along with each other.

10
Your 1st Job

Hey, by this time and stage of your life, you're probably starting to think of having some decent amount of cash on hand so that you can purchase things you want without asking your mom for cash frequently. With that being said, let's starting thinking about that 1st job you're going to land! When trying to get your first job, how about considering locations, how

Life's Lil Journeys

far it is away from school and home, so that you can get transportation to and from without causing logistical troubles or issues.

Think about something you would like to do and not simply doing it for the money. Remember all money is not good money and when doing something you like or love, the money will follow. This is a statement that will hold true later on in life when you start deciding on your career choice. So, find a job you would enjoy going to, be on time, work as if you don't need the money. Learn things so that you can use those skills later on in life. Be a team player. Volunteer to do things that others are hesitant or reluctant to do. This will show employers that you're eager to learn and willing to take on more responsibility.

11
Financial Management

Money, that's right! That good ole dollar bill. I once heard someone say having enough money is like having air to breathe. When you have it and enough of it you tend to not worry and stress about things or making ends meet. Financial management is simply managing your money. Having a monthly budget, knowing how much you have coming in and how much

Life's Lil Journeys

going out. By taking control and being in control of your finances, life seems to be less complicated and easy to manage. Try not to look at it as being a tight wad or stingy. However, you are being in control of your spending habits and learning how to control your thoughts about money.

Remember, money is like a tool. When using the right tool for the job, you get things done in a sometime quick and efficient manner and then there are times when saving your money takes a little bit longer. However, you have taught yourself patience and can pay cash for what you want. As a teenager/almost adult, if you start learning and teaching yourself good financial habits, you will have accumulated a good size savings account that you could use at your discretion at a later date in life. Remember the key here is manage, control your spending, and save your money. It's like investing in yourself. There's no one who's going to handle your money situations like you would. And on another note, let's talk about loaning and borrowing money.

Financial Management

My father shared with me, if you have something to give, then give it, especially when it comes to family members. But don't expect it back, otherwise you're going to cause yourself unnecessary heartache and pain. He would also go on to say, "The word NO is a complete sentence!" If you're going to loan someone a significant amount of money, make out an *I Owe You* note, and have them sign it. It might cause them to think twice about borrowing and hurting a relationship. When it comes to money, people act funny. Keep your friendships true and real. When and if you have to ask for a loan, be a man of your word and pay it back, as promised. If something comes up, let that person know ahead of time and try to work out an alternative plan. The key note here is "Being true to thy self."

12
Continuing Your Education

Remember when you first started learning things in school, life and in general, how exciting and sometimes fearful that could be. Well, let's close this out on a positive note. I'm talking about taking everything that you have learned so far, and putting it to use to better your outlook and position in life. Maybe you have plans for being an entrepreneur (business owner) and possibly furthering your education through attending college. Heck, you may want to learn a skill or trade.

Financial Management

The options at this juncture of your life are endless. Available to you because you have given yourself opportunity, by keeping and staying out of trouble and out of harm's way. When opportunity and preparedness cross paths, then you may have what some would consider luck. How about calling it, "Being in the right place at the right time?"

Whatever the case may be, you are developing into being your own man. By continuing your education, you will learn many different things that can and will help you be successful in your future adventures and endeavors. Take time to get to know you, your weakness and strengths, polish yourself up and sharpen your skills continuously.

Life will open many doors, just because you have given and taken the time and made many sacrifices. Show your gratitude, appreciation, humbleness and willingness, listen and learn from **<u>HER/ YOUR MOM!</u>**

Conclusion

*There you have it… life's little journeys.
Enjoy your reading, as well as your life ahead.*

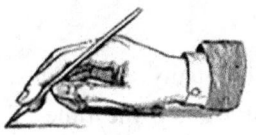

Written by: *Melvin J. Stevenson*

About the Author

MELVIN J. STEVENSON - SMSGT-E8, RET 33yrs - USAFR; US Postal Service, RET 37yrs – AZ; Valley Big Brother Big Sister, 25yrs.

Melvin was born in Philadelphia, PA in 1963. He moved to New Jersey and graduated from CCVTS, Pennsauken, NJ. in 1981. Mel joined the US Air Force, traveled and enjoyed many parts of the world.

About the Author

Mel's first book ***Life's Lil Journeys*** comes from life experiences. He has served his country and has had a great second career with the US Postal Service. Mel loves to work with youth which is evident by his tireless volunteering for the Valley Big Brother Big Sister organization. Mel is looking forward to writing other motivational books in his future endeavors.

www.ingramcontent.com/pod-product-compliance
Lightning Source LLC
Chambersburg PA
CBHW071545080526
44588CB00011B/1802